Y0-CLG-131

PETS

A REFERENCE
FIRST BOOK

BY LEDA BLUMBERG

A GROLIER COMPANY

FRANKLIN WATTS
NEW YORK | LONDON | TORONTO
SYDNEY | 1983

Photographs courtesy of:
Creszentia Allen: pp. 3, 39, 47, 55;
The American Kennel Gazette:
pp. 4, 6, 9, 32, 57, 59;
D.J. Herda: pp. 11, 12, 16, 22, 27, 29, 30,
31, 33, 35, 36, 46, 52, 54, 62, 64;
no credit: p. 17; Ed Peterson: p. 38;
Michael Einbinder: p. 40.

Cover photographs courtesy of D.J. Herda:
top left, top right, bottom left, bottom right;
Creszentia Allen: top center.

Library of Congress Cataloging in Publication Data

Blumberg, Leda.
Pets.

(A Reference first book)
Summary: A dictionary format describes a variety
of pets, and includes advice on pet care.
1. Pets—Dictionaries, Juvenile
[1. Pets—Dictionaries] I. Title. II. Series.
SF416.B58 1983   636.08'87'0321   83-1347
ISBN 0-531-04649-4

PETS

———

Because they let me raise lambs in the basement,
goats on the porch, and horses in the backyard,
this book is lovingly dedicated to my parents.

———

AUTHOR'S NOTE

Owning a pet can be one of life's greatest pleasures. It is a chance to love and care for a living creature. By watching its growth and observing its behavior, you will discover that a pet can be exciting, amusing, and enlightening.

Each type of pet needs different care. Some pets are easy to look after, while others are difficult and demanding. Pets aren't toys, and a certain amount of work, some unpleasant, is involved in properly caring for them. You must be willing to devote part of every day to meeting your animal's needs.

All pets, whether tiny mice or huge Saint Bernards, depend upon their owners for food, housing, warmth, protection, and health care. Love, although it is very important, is not enough.

Pet keeping began about ten thousand years ago when dogs were first domesticated. In ancient Egypt dogs and cats were considered sacred. Pharaohs filled their gardens with monkeys, baboons, and antelope. In Rome citizens enjoyed swans, peacocks, and a variety of singing and talking birds. Their emperors preferred more exotic pets like lions and tigers. Powdered with gold dust, their sharp teeth and claws removed, these animals slept at their masters' feet.

During the Middle Ages both nobles and peasants owned hounds, cats, monkeys, and falcons. Europe's kings kept all kinds of birds, including storks, in jeweled gold and silver cages.

Today a vast variety of nature's creatures are loved and cared for in millions of homes.

A

ABYSSINIAN CATS. These cats closely resemble the mummified remains of cats from ancient Egypt. They are originally from the upper Nile Valley and are probably the closest living link to the first domestic cats.

Abyssinians are either a ruddy brown ticked with darker shades of brown and black, or brick red ticked with chocolate brown. Unlike many domestic cats, they seem to enjoy playing in water and swimming. They are affectionate, intelligent, and playful pets. *See also* CATS.

Abyssinian cat

Afghan hound

AFGHAN HOUNDS. Afghans are tall, elegant dogs that originated in ancient Egypt about five thousand years ago. They were later bred in Afghanistan to hunt big game like leopards and gazelles. Afghans are among the swiftest of all dogs. If given ample room for exercise, they make excellent pets. Their long, silky coats need plenty of grooming. *See also* DOGS.

AMPHIBIANS. Amphibians spend part of their lives in water and part of their lives on land. Most amphibians lay their eggs in water. Young amphibians breathe through gills and live like fish. Eventually they grow legs and develop lungs so that they can breathe air and live on land. Some amphibians return to water only to mate; others live in the water all the time.

Frogs, toads, and salamanders are amphibians that can be kept as pets. *See also* FROGS AND TOADS; SALAMANDERS; and TADPOLES.

ANTS. Ants live in highly organized groups called *colonies*. Each ant has its own special job within the colony. Worker ants build the nest, add new tunnels, gather food, care for the young, and defend the colony. Drones, or male ants, mate with the queen and then die. Queen ants do nothing except lay eggs— often thousands a day. There is usually only one queen to a colony, but some colonies have more.

Housing. You can buy an ant farm, or you can make your own. Ants can be kept in a jar filled with soil and covered with cheesecloth. Place a block of wood in the soil in the middle of the jar. The ants will build tunnels through the soil surrounding the wood. You can watch them through the glass.

Because ants build their nest in darkness, keep the farm covered with a dark cloth and remove it only when you watch them. You can use a magnifying glass to observe these fascinating creatures. An ant farm should be kept at room temperature, away from radiators and out of the sun. Moisten the soil with a few drops of water every day.

To collect ants for your farm, dig up an ant hill and take the soil containing ant eggs, larvae, adult ants, and a queen. Without a queen, your colony will soon die because she alone lays fertile eggs for future ant generations. A queen is larger than the other ants and is often found near the bottom of the nest.

Feeding. Ants eat all kinds of food. Feed them bits of fruits, vegetables, bread crumbs, cereal, table scraps, and dead insects. A small piece of cardboard makes a good feeding dish. Feed your ants every other day, and remove leftovers before they spoil. Pet ants can drink water from moisture in the soil or from a dampened sponge placed on top of the soil. *See also* INSECTS.

B

BALINESE CATS. Long-haired Siamese cats, Balinese were developed by inbreeding Siamese cats that were born with long hair. *See also* CATS.

BASSET HOUNDS. These short-legged, long-bodied hounds were developed centuries ago as hunting dogs for French nobility. A basset has a ''nose'' second only to that of a bloodhound. Bassets are used to hunt rabbit, squir-

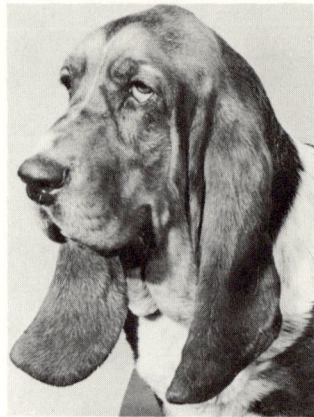

Basset hound

rels, foxes, pheasant, and other small game. Their short legs enable them to hunt in thick underbrush without losing the scent. They are friendly, docile, intelligent dogs and are good with children. *See also* DOGS.

BEAGLES. These small, multicolored hunting dogs hunt both singly and in packs. Because they are gentle and affectionate, beagles make good pets. However, they tend to bay (howl) at night. *See also* DOGS.

BIRDS. Over the centuries breeders have developed countless varieties of singing and ornamental birds, many with gorgeous plumage and glorious voices. Most of our pet birds originally came from countries other than the United States. At one time birds were imported in enormous quantities. As a result of overcrowding and mistreatment, large numbers died. Because of this the government passed laws restricting imports and demanding decent standards for the care of birds. Nevertheless, about one million birds are smuggled into the United States every year. Therefore, before buying, make sure your future pet is healthy.

A young bird becomes easily attached to its owner and is easier to tame than an older bird. Choose your bird carefully, because it may be with you for many years.

Housing. Birds need roomy cages. Small birds, like canaries, should have room to fly from perch to perch. Large birds, like parrots, need space to flap their wings. Cages should be kept out of drafts. Tropical birds chill easily and could become ill or die. Cage covers (a towel can be used as a cover) are useful to stop drafts and to keep birds quiet at night. Birds stop singing, chattering, and twittering when it is dark.

Each cage should be equipped with perches, food and water dispensers, a piece of cuttlebone or mineral block, and a block of wood for chewing. (Cuttlebone isn't bone; it is a piece of shell from a cuttlefish. By pecking on it, birds keep their beaks trim and get calcium, which is important in their diet.)

The cage floor should be covered with newspapers and sprinkled with sand. Because they don't have teeth, birds need sand or grit to grind food inside their stomachs.

If you are interested in keeping several birds or in breeding birds, you need an aviary. Aviaries are large indoor or outdoor screened structures. They should be securely built to protect your feathered pets from dogs, cats, and other animals. Aviaries for tropical birds must always be kept warm. Because some birds fight with other kinds of birds, be sure to house only those that get along with each other. Before bringing a new bird into an aviary, isolate it for two weeks to be sure it isn't carrying a disease.

Feeding. Most bird foods are mixtures of seeds and vitamins. In addition to commercial foods, feed your bird fresh fruits and vegetables. Wash greens to clean off harmful insecticides.

All birds molt. They shed their feathers periodically and then grow new ones. When molting, birds need insects, mealworms, or high-protein bird foods. They also need this extra nourishment when breeding or raising young.

Care. Remove droppings from the cage every day. Many cages have removable trays on the bottom which can be taken out and cleaned. Wash the entire cage with warm water and disinfectant every few months.

Birds must have fresh food and water daily. Never allow food to stay in the cage long enough to spoil.

Give your pets a chance to bathe several times a week. A bowl filled with water,, a misting with a bird or plant sprayer, or the kitchen sink with the faucet dripping, are all good bird baths.

Let your bird out of its cage to exercise every few days. Cover windows and mirrors so your bird doesn't fly into them and become injured. And, of course, close all doors. Tidbits of food can be used to entice your pet back into its cage. You can have your bird's wing feathers clipped to restrict flying. Your veterinarian or pet-store manager can do this for you.

In the wild, birds keep their beaks and claws trimmed by using them on nuts, seeds, and rough branches. Caged birds must be given hard materials for chewing and proper perches for gripping.

Some birds need to have their beaks and claws trimmed periodically at a veterinarian's office or at a pet shop.

Taming. Birds are timid and frighten easily. Therefore, taming must be done slowly and gently. Tempt your pet with food you hold in your hand. Eventually, your bird will perch on your finger and eat. Taming outside the cage is easiest if the bird's wing feathers are clipped.

Some birds, like parrots and mynas, can be taught to "talk" when they hear words and phrases repeated over and over again. (They are mimics and don't really know what they are saying.) Many pet stores sell records and tapes to help you teach your bird to talk.

Health. Some signs of illness are diarrhea, nasal discharge, ruffled feathers, loss of appetite, and listlessness. Should you suspect that your bird is ill, call your veterinarian. *See also* CANARIES; FINCHES; LOVEBIRDS; MYNA BIRDS; PARAKEETS; PARROTS; and PIGEONS.

BIRMAN CATS. Birmans are known as the sacred cats of Burma. At one time they resided in Buddhist temples. People believed they were reincarnations of Burmese priests.

These round-faced, stocky cats have long, silky hair and white paws. They are intelligent and affectionate. *See also* CATS.

BULLDOGS. Also called English bulldogs, these dogs may look mean and ferocious, but they are actually friendly and even tempered. They were originally bred for the sport of fighting and killing bulls. Today bulldogs are bred to be gentle, devoted, sweet-natured pets. *See also* DOGS.

Bulldog

BURMESE CATS. All Burmese cats were bred and developed in the United States from a single female cat, "Wong Mau," who was brought to America in the 1930s. They have short, satiny, brown hair and brilliant golden eyes and are intelligent and playful. *See also* CATS.

C

CANARIES. The canary is a type of finch that originally came from the Canary Islands. Some kinds have been bred for their beautiful songs; others for their gorgeous feathers. Canaries may be yellow, blue, orange, red, pink, or patterned.

If you want a singing canary, be sure to buy a male, and not one that's silent (some are). Females twirp and twitter but do not sing. Listen to your future pet's song before you buy. *See also* BIRDS.

CATERPILLARS (Butterflies and Moths). A wormlike caterpillar changing into a beautiful winged butterfly or moth is one of nature's miracles.

To witness this miracle, bring home a caterpillar with some of the leaves it was feeding on when you found it. This is important because many caterpillars eat only one type of leaf. Place your caterpillar with the leaves, soil, and twigs in a box or jar. Cover the container with cheesecloth. Add fresh leaves every day for your caterpillar's meals.

A moth caterpillar spins a silk *cocoon* around itself. A butterfly caterpillar develops a hard-shelled skin called a *chrysalis*. Your caterpillar may spend a few days or several months inside its case while its body changes. Cocoons and chrysalises need moist air. Therefore, place some wet paper in a corner of the container. One day the case will split open, and a lovely winged creature will emerge.

Butterflies and moths should not be handled. Their wings are covered with tiny scales that rub off on your hands. It is best to return your newly emerged butterfly or moth to the wild. *See also* INSECTS.

Black swallowtail butterfly

CATS. Worshiped as gods, tortured as demons! Cats were first domesticated in ancient Egypt about 5,000 years ago. Because the Egyptians considered them gods, killing cats was a crime punishable by death. When a cat died, its body was mummified and buried in a richly decorated case. Sometimes mummified mice were entombed with a cat as food for its "afterlife." Owners of a deceased cat shaved off their eyebrows as a sign of mourning.

The ancient Chinese also worshiped cats. First introduced to China to protect silkworm cocoons from rodents, cats soon became cherished. Special rites and ceremonies were held in their honor.

During the Middle Ages superstitious people in Europe detested cats. They associated them with evil and believed that the creatures were demons serving the Devil and his witches. Many cats were tortured and burned alive.

At one time people used to seal a living cat into the foundation of a building for good luck. Even today superstitions about cats abound. In the United States it is often considered bad luck if a black cat crosses your path. In England, however, black cats are thought to bring good luck.

**Short-haired
American cat**

Today cats are the most popular of all house pets. Their beauty, grace, and affectionate, yet aloof ways endear them to their owners. Cats amuse and sometimes annoy with their endless antics and their leave-me-alone attitude. They can't be trained the way you train a dog.

Finding a kitten or cat isn't difficult. Animal shelters, pet stores, cat breeders, neighbors, and friends often have kittens in need of homes. Occasionally a homeless cat will find you.

Housing. A kitten needs a cushion or cat bed. Eventually it will choose its own sleeping spots, but it should be offered a bed of its own. Kittens and cats need two dishes: one for food and one for water. These should be easy to clean and designed so that they won't tip over easily.

All cats scratch in order to keep their claws sharp. To save your furniture, buy or make a scratching post, which is usually a carpeted post standing on a firm base. Some people nail burlap to a basement wall, or supply a log for catclawing.

A litter box filled with commercial cat litter, sawdust, or wood shavings makes a perfect bathroom for an indoor cat. Kittens soon learn to use their litter box every time "nature calls." Remove droppings from the litter box every day and change the litter twice a week.

Your playful kitten will enjoy toys. Pieces of string, Ping-pong balls, crumpled paper, and empty spools are ideal. Toys stuffed with catnip are a special treat. Catnip is an herb whose mintlike scent excites cats and makes them extraordinarily playful.

Feeding. When kittens are six to eight weeks old, mother cats wean them, and human "mothers" must take over. Young kittens need three or four meals a day. Their stomachs are about the size of a walnut and can hold only a small amount of food at one time. Grown cats eat one or two meals a day. Feed your cat at the same time and in the same place. Keep clean, fresh water in a dish day and night.

A good basic diet consists of two-thirds dry cat chow mixed with one-third canned fish or meat. Kitchen leftovers such as vegetables, milk, cheese, eggs, and meat can be added to commercial cat foods. Don't give your pet fish or chicken bones because these could splinter and stick in its throat. Kittens can have milk, but older cats often have trouble digesting it. Wheat-germ oil, cod-liver oil, or vegetable oil should be added to your cat's food once a week. Oil is good for digestion and keeps the fur shining.

Even if your cat is a mighty hunter, it still must be fed a well-balanced diet. Withholding food from cats doesn't make them better "mousers." Actually, proper diet keeps them in shape to chase and catch prey.

Health. When choosing a kitten or cat, look for an animal with a thick, shiny coat. Bald spots, rashes, and scabs are signs of poor health. Eyes, nose, and ears should be clear and not runny. Kittens shouldn't be skinny or overly fat. Healthy kittens are always playful.

Take your new cat to a veterinarian to be inoculated against rabies and distemper and checked for worms. A secure, well-ventilated cat carrier may be necessary for taking your pet to the veterinarian.

Neutering: Have your cat neutered if you don't intend to breed cats. There are far too many homeless cats. Simple operations, called *altering* for males and *spaying* for females, will prevent litters of unwanted kittens. Neutering is usually done when a cat is between six and eight months old.

Declawing: If your cat scratches furniture, you can have its front claws removed. However, keep in mind that declawing leaves your cat unable to catch prey, climb trees, or protect itself. This operation should be performed only on cats that never go outside. Declawing is not recommended for most cats.

Fleas: Fleas get their nourishment from the blood of animals. They're superb hoppers that can quickly swarm over your pet. To prevent fleas, there are defleaing powders, sprays, and shampoos on the market. Commercial flea collars are not recommended because they usually contain harmful chemicals. Once your cat is free of fleas, be sure to clean its bedding, or a new batch of fleas may infest your pet.

Grooming. A comb and brush are necessary to keep your cat groomed. Although cats spend a great deal of time licking and grooming themselves, loose hairs do build up. When the loose hairs are licked and swallowed, they can form harmful *hair balls* in your pet's stomach that can make it ill.

Choosing a Cat. Of the more than thirty recognized cat breeds, the most popular are listed in this book. Cat shows are excellent places to view the different breeds and see which ones you like. *See also* ABYSSINIAN CATS; BALINESE CATS; BIRMAN CATS; BURMESE CATS; DOMESTIC SHORTHAIR CATS (HOUSE CATS); HIMALAYAN CATS; KORAT CATS; MAINE COON CATS; MANX CATS; PERSIAN CATS; REX CATS; RUSSIAN BLUE CATS; and SIAMESE CATS.

CHICKENS. Three thousand years ago the Egyptians and Chinese kept and bred domestic fowl. The Egyptians incubated eggs in nests made of heated bricks. Throughout history many varieties of chickens have been developed. Some have fluffy, feathery hats, others have fuzzy pantaloons, and still others have multicolored feathers and bodies with decorative patterns.

Chickens are not intelligent, responsive pets, but they can be rewarding. Hens will supply you with plenty of fresh eggs. A good laying hen can produce more than two hundred eggs per year.

Hens make better pets than roosters. Roosters can be noisy, aggressive, and ever ready to fight each other. However, they are reliable alarm clocks that announce dawn each morning.

Some communities don't allow chickens in backyards, so check your local laws before buying any. Even if they are permitted, be considerate. Neighbors may not appreciate the noise of clucking hens and crowing roosters.

Housing. Chickens need a securely fenced-in area with a weatherproof coop. The fence should be 6 feet (1.8 m) high and sunk 2 feet (.6 m) in the ground to keep your chickens safe from predators such as foxes, raccoon, and dogs.

Coops should allow at least 3 to 4 square feet (about 1 sq m) per bird. They should contain nesting boxes filled with hay, perches for roosting, a water container, a feeding trough, and a container for grit. Be sure the feed and water containers are large enough to accommodate all birds, or there's bound to be trouble. The coop should be bedded with clean, fresh straw or wood shavings.

If you buy very young chicks, keep them indoors in a box heated with a lamp. Cover the bottom of the box with paper sprinkled with grit, and supply food and water dishes.

Feeding. Commercial chicken feed consisting of grains and seeds makes a good basic diet. You can add greens, such as lawn clippings or table scraps. Occasionally sprinkle bone meal or crushed oyster shell on food. These provide extra calcium that prevents eggshells from becoming thin and brittle.

Chickens can be given food in troughs inside their houses or on the ground outside. Ground feeding encourages scratching. Chickens enjoy scratching through dirt and then rolling in it. That's their way of bathing!

Chickens need grit because they don't have teeth. Grit is used in their stomachs to grind food.

Health. Regular care, clean, well-ventilated housing, and good food help prevent most diseases. Seek advice from a local chicken farmer or from your feedstore if you suspect that you have a sick chicken.

CHIHUAHUAS. Members of the smallest of all dog breeds, chihuahuas are so tiny that one can be tucked away in a woman's handbag. They are about 5 inches (12.7 cm) high at the shoulder and weigh between 1 and 6 pounds (.45 and 2.7 kg). Chihuahuas originally came from the state of Chihuahua, Mexico. They are very delicate and timid and, therefore, aren't good pets for children. *See also* DOGS.

COCKER SPANIELS. The cocker spaniel was originally trained to hunt woodcock. That's why it is called "cocker." Today it is a favorite show dog and an ideal family pet. *See also* DOGS.

COLLIES. Originally used for herding livestock, collies guarded large flocks of sheep day and night. These beautiful dogs need lots of exercise and regular grooming to keep their long coats in good shape. Some collies are nervous and will nip if bothered. *See also* DOGS.

CRICKETS. Kept as pets for centuries, especially in the Orient, crickets are believed to bring good luck. Emperors used to keep crickets in elaborate cages made of ivory and jade, hoping that their pets would bring them peace and happiness.

Grasshopper

In Asia crickets were also kept for sport. Male crickets fought each other while people watched and placed bets on their favorite insect.

Crickets have also been kept because of their musical chirping. Only males chirp. Their sounds attract females and frighten other males away. Wings, not vocal chords, make the sounds. A scraper under the upper wing rubs against a file on the lower wing to create the familiar chirp.

Housing. Crickets can be housed in a jar or a small glass tank. Place sand on the bottom and add twigs and leaves for shelter. Cover the top with cheesecloth so that your crickets won't leap out. Keep the cage out of bright sunlight, and sprinkle the sand with a few drops of water every other day. Don't keep two males together, or they will fight. (Males have two long spikes at the ends of their abdomens; females have three.)

Feeding. Feed your crickets a variety of foods, like small bits of vegetables, fruits, bread crumbs, and insects. A moist sponge or damp piece of cotton will provide drinking water.

Note: Grasshoppers can also be kept as pets. They require the same care as crickets. *See also INSECTS.*

D

DACHSHUNDS. These small, short-legged hounds were bred in Germany to hunt badgers. Their long, low build is perfect for burrowing deep into badger holes. Although their legs are short, they are fast runners and courageous hunters. Dachshunds should be trained at an early age because they tend to be stubborn. They make enjoyable pets and are alert watchdogs. *See also* DOGS.

Dachshund

DALMATIANS. Easily recognized by their sleek white coats spotted with dark brown or black, dalmations were once called "coach dogs" because they accompanied and protected horse-drawn carriages. They scared off bandits and drove wolves away from horses. Dalmatians serve as mascots for many American firehouses. They make affectionate, loyal pets. *See also* DOGS.

DOBERMAN PINSCHERS. Because Doberman pinschers are smart and strong, they are trained as guard dogs, police dogs, and army dogs. They can also make devoted pets. Many Doberman pinschers have their tails docked and their ears cropped. Because ear cropping is painful, it is illegal in many states. *See also* DOGS.

DOGS. Ever since early times, dogs have played a role in human lives. They were probably first domesticated when early people brought wild puppies into their homes and trained them to help hunt.

Dogs have proved their usefulness as hunters, protectors, and herders. They learned to pull sleds for Eskimo, herd livestock for shepherds, track animals for hunters, and defend property for people all over the world. They guide the blind, aid the deaf, and entertain with tricks as circus performers. Best of all, they are loving companions capable of becoming attached and devoted to their owners. A dog can, indeed, be a best friend.

Dogs make wonderful pets, but they are a serious responsibility. They depend upon their owners for food, housing, exercise, grooming, training, and veterinary care. Their food and medical needs can be expensive. However, the relationship that develops between a caring person and a devoted dog is worth the expense.

Housing. Every dog needs a place of its own: a blanket, cushion, or dogbed inside, or a doghouse outside. A doghouse should be well built and weather-tight. Use straw, blankets, or a cushion in the doghouse, and clean this bedding from time to time.

Outdoor kennels are suitable for working dogs, hunting dogs, and guard dogs, but animals that always live outside usually aren't as affectionate as house dogs.

Unless you live in the country away from major roads, your dog should be confined when it is alone outside. A fenced-in yard, a dog run, or a strong lead attached to an overhead line works well.

Any dog can be tempted to stray. Male dogs often travel miles to track down females in heat. Be sure your dog wears a collar with identification and rabies tags.

Feeding. Use dry dog chow mixed with canned dog food. Add vegetables, grains, cheese, potatoes, or eggs. Wheat germ, cod-liver, or vegetable oil can be added to give your dog's coat a healthy shine. Vitamin supplements usually aren't needed if your pet is fed a proper diet.

Young puppies need three or four meals each day. At four to six months of age, two meals a day are enough. When fully grown, at one to one and a half years old, one meal a day is sufficient. Feed your dog at the same time every day. If you switch brands of dog food, do so gradually. Sudden changes in diet can make your pet sick. Clean, fresh water should always be handy for your pet.

Dogs love bones, but give only shin bones or large knuckle bones. Other bones splinter and can get caught in your animal's throat. Rawhide "bones" provide excellent chewing without ever splintering.

Grooming. Whether your dog's hair is curly, shaggy, silky, or short, it will need to be brushed or combed periodically. Brushing removes dead hair and dirt. It also gives you a chance to check your dog for cuts, insect bites, and parasites like fleas and ticks.

Fleas leave black, gritty deposits on your animal's skin and make your pet very itchy. Shampoos, powders, and sprays that kill fleas are available. Flea collars are not recommended because they contain poisons that make some dogs sick. To prevent fleas from coming back, your dog's bedding should also be cleaned and "defleaed." Adding Brewer's yeast to your dog's diet is thought to help prevent fleas. Add one tablespoonful a day for small dogs, two tablespoons for large ones.

Ticks are blood-sucking insects that attach themselves to animals. Ticks' bodies swell up like tiny balloons when they have their fill of blood. These pests should be removed carefully. Use tweezers, making sure you pull the entire tick out. Dab alcohol on the bite. Never attempt to burn ticks off.

Poodles and several other breeds often have their fur clipped by a dog groomer. Clipping isn't necessary; it's just a matter of fashion.

Bathe your dog when he's very dirty or has fleas. Use gentle soap or dog shampoo with warm water. After bathing and rinsing your pet, rub it with towels to help it dry off. Most dogs keep their nails trim by running around. However, if your pet's nails grow too long, have them clipped. Your veterinarian can do this when your dog has its yearly inoculations.

Health. Take a new pet to your veterinarian for inoculations and a thorough examination. Once each year your dog will need shots against distemper, rabies, and other illnesses, and each spring a checkup for heartworms (a type of worm that affects the heart).

Every few months have your dog checked for intestinal worms. Only a veterinarian should deworm your pet. Over-the-counter preparations and home remedies aren't always safe or effective. Common signs of illness are: loss of appetite, diarrhea, excessive vomiting, limping, and crying.

If you have no intention of breeding your dog, have it *neutered* so that it can't reproduce. Your vet can perform this operation when your dog is about six months old. Females that are not neutered (spayed) go into heat twice a year and attract a crowd of barking admirers.

Training. Every dog should go through basic training and learn to *sit, lie down, stay, heel*, and *come*. Training begins when a puppy is about three months old. Have short daily sessions. When your pet does what you wish, reward it with food, a kind word, and affection. Repetition and patience! That's the way to teach.

Teach your dog to walk quietly by your side. Use a *choke collar*—one that tightens when you pull on it—and gently tug on it every time your dog pulls away. Say "heel" to keep it by your side. Say "sit" and press down on its rump to teach it to sit. After "sit," the next lesson is "down." When your dog is sitting, gently pull its forelegs forward until it's flat on the ground and say "down."

Teach your dog to come when called. You can start teaching "come" on a long leash, and as your dog learns, continue the lessons when it is off the leash. Reward it every time it comes. Next, teach "stay." When your pet is sitting, say "stay" and gradually move away. Every time your dog starts to move, correct it, and repeat the "stay" command. At first, make your pup stay for a few seconds, then gradually increase the amount of time. Don't lose patience, and remember that your tone of voice means more to your dog than the actual words.

If you've never trained a dog, it's a good idea to enroll yourself and your dog in a dog obedience class.

About housebreaking: It usually isn't difficult because dogs don't like to soil near their beds. In nature wild dogs never mess inside their dens. After a pup is weaned from its mother, confine it to a small area that is covered with newspapers. Your pet will soon use only one corner as a bathroom, so you'll only need to paper a small area. To teach your dog to use the outdoors, take him outside immediately after meals, naps, and playtime. Your dog will soon learn to use the great outdoors, not the living room rug. If your dog messes indoors, say "no" in a firm voice, then take it outdoors immediately. Rubbing its nose in its mess will not teach your dog any faster.

Choosing a dog. There are about two hundred breeds of domestic dogs. The variety is vast and astonishing. There are enormous Saint Bernards, tiny chihuahuas, furry sheepdogs, and curly-haired poodles.

Mongrels, dogs of mixed breeds, can make excellent pets. "Mutts" are easy to locate through newspapers, at dog pounds, and in pet shops. Although they are usually free, remember that their care and feeding will cost as much as high-priced purebreds. Before purchasing a pet, have a vet examine the animal.

The American Kennel Club is an organization that was formed to encourage an interest in purebred dogs. It classifies dogs into six basic groups: sporting, hound, terrier, working, toy, and nonsporting.

Sporting dogs were originally developed as hunting dogs to find and retrieve game birds. *Hounds* were bred to hunt by sight or ground scent. *Terriers* were used to hunt by digging into soil to reach burrowing animals.

Working dogs were developed to handle various jobs, like herding, sled pulling, and guarding. *Toy dogs* were bred primarily for pleasure and companionship. Many toy dogs are simply tiny versions of larger breeds. *Nonsporting dogs* are dogs that don't quite fit into any of the above categories. They are bred for a variety of uses. The most popular dog breeds are listed below. *See also* AFGHAN HOUNDS, BASSET HOUNDS, BEAGLES, BULLDOGS, CHIHUA-HUAS, COCKER SPANIELS, COLLIES, DACHSHUNDS, DALMATIANS, DOBER-MAN PINSCHERS, ENGLISH SPRINGER SPANIELS, FOX TERRIERS, GERMAN SHEPHERDS, GOLDEN RETRIEVERS, GREAT DANES, GREYHOUNDS, IRISH SETTERS, LABRADOR RETRIEVERS, LHASA APSOS, NEWFOUNDLANDS, PEKINGESE, POINTERS, POODLES, SAINT BERNARDS, SCHNAUZERS, SCOTTISH TERRIERS, SHETLAND SHEEPDOGS, SHIH TZUS, SIBERIAN HUS-KIES, and YORKSHIRE TERRIERS.

DOMESTIC SHORTHAIR CATS (COMMON HOUSE CAT). Domestic short-hairs, the ever popular *house cats* or *alley cats*, are well known everywhere. Their variety of coat colors and patterns is endless. They first came to the United States on the *Mayflower* with the Pilgrims and earned their keep protecting grain from mice and rats. Their popularity as pets and "mousers" is apparent all over the world. *See also* CATS.

DONKEYS. Donkeys can be gentle and affectionate pets. They need a securely fenced-in pasture with a run-in shed for shelter from wind, rain, sun, and flies. Be sure that they always have a supply of clean, fresh drinking water and a salt block to lick. Grain and hay are essential when the pasture is not lush and during the winter months when grass has stopped growing.

Like horses and ponies, they must be looked after daily. They need their hooves trimmed, they must be wormed regularly, and they need vaccinations in the spring. *See also* HORSES.

DUCKS. These birds can become tame pets. Young ducklings sometimes become so attached to their owners that they follow them around. Because ducks like company, keep more than one. Have their wing feathers clipped to keep them from flying away.

Housing. Ducks need a small pond for swimming and a fenced-in area or an enclosed shelter for protection from animals like dogs and foxes. Be sure your ducks have small trees or shrubs for shade and nesting. Place nesting boxes filled with hay in safe secluded places. If your pond freezes over in winter, provide your ducks with a small shelter. Cover the floor with a layer of clean hay, and change it when it becomes messy.

Feeding. Ducks living on natural ponds find most of their own food, but by giving them duck pellets, you keep them tame. During the winter they need to be fed because there isn't enough food in the frozen outdoors. Set out buckets of drinking water for them when the pond turns to ice.

Ducks

E-F

ENGLISH SPRINGER SPANIELS. These dogs are playful, spirited companions. They can be taught to retrieve game both on land and in water. These gentle, lively pets need lots of exercise outdoors. *See also* DOGS.

FINCHES. There are many different kinds of finches that vary in color, size, and behavior. Finches are sociable birds and, therefore, happiest when kept in pairs. They eat small seeds and greens, and they need grit and cuttlebone. Some finches eat insects. They enjoy bathing and should have clean bath water daily. *See also* BIRDS.

FISH. These come in an endless variety of sizes, shapes, and colors. Although you can't touch or play with them, they are fun to watch.

Pet stores give you fish in water-filled plastic bags. Each bag has enough oxygen for about one hour, so take your fish home immediately. Place the plastic bag containing the fish in your aquarium. This allows the water temperature in the bag to adjust slowly to the water temperature in the tank. Sudden temperature changes kill fish. After about half an hour, slit the bag open and let your fish swim into its new home.

Never pick up a fish with your hands. A fish's body is covered with protective mucus. When you touch it, some of the mucus wipes off and may cause your pet to develop a hard-to-cure infection. Use a dipper or soft net to move your fish.

Don't tap on your fish tank. Most fish don't hear well, but they are sensitive to vibrations. Tapping on the side of a fish tank causes water vibrations that hit the fish like shock waves.

Housing. An aquarium that is properly set up is a beautiful miniature world. Glass tanks with stainless steel sides make the best aquariums because more surface water is exposed to air than in round fishbowls and oxygen enters water through the surface. Fish need oxygen, so you don't want your tank to be too small or overcrowded. A shortage of oxygen leads to disease and dead fish. One gallon of water for each inch (2.54 cm) of fish is a good general rule.

Prepare your aquarium one week before you buy your fish. This gives water time to "age" so that all the chlorine can evaporate, and it gives you time to check the condition of your air pump, filter, and water heater.

Be sure to choose a good spot for your aquarium because after it's filled with water, it will be too heavy to move. Place your tank near, but not in front of, a window. Direct sunlight may overheat the water and cook your pet. If your tank is in a dark area, you can use artificial lights.

To prepare your tank, wash it with a salt solution and water. *Never use soap*. Any trace of soap can kill fish. Rinse the gravel you will use for the bottom until the water runs clear. *Never use pebbles you have collected outside*. They may contain harmful bacteria.

When the tank is clean, place the gravel on the bottom. Build up the gravel so that it's higher in the back of the tank, and slopes downward toward the front. This allows wastes and leftover food to drift to the front, where it can be easily removed. *Don't use glass gravel* because fish can cut their mouths on it while they are eating.

Place a few plants toward the back of the tank. Plants look attractive, provide shelter for shy fish, and offer breeding fish a place to lay their eggs. They also serve as natural filters that help to keep the water clean and produce oxygen for your fish to breathe. *Never collect plants from streams and brooks*. They may have bacteria or insects that make fish sick. Buy greenery at your pet store.

Your tank should have an air pump for putting more oxygen in the water; a filter to keep the water clean; and a heater with a thermostat to regulate the water temperature. A thermometer in your tank enables you to check the water temperature daily. Fish can die if the water gets too hot or too cold. Because they are cold-blooded, their body heat is determined by the temperature of the water around them.

If you are setting up a saltwater aquarium, mix sea-salt mixture (from a pet store) with water and allow it to age for one week. If you collect seawater from an ocean, let it stand for three weeks before using it.

Keep a cover on your tank to keep fish from accidentally jumping out and to keep curious animals like cats and dogs from coming in.

Use a hand siphon to suck dirt out of your aquarium. If your tank has a filter, it will need cleaning every two to four weeks. Tanks without filters must be siphoned out every few days. Keep a supply of aged water handy, and add some to your tank once a week. Clean your aquarium thoroughly two or three times a year.

Feeding. Some fish need one, others need two feedings a day. Give your fish all they can eat, and after about ten minutes remove any uneaten food or it will rot, foul the water, and make your fish sick. Overeating is a major cause of death among aquarium pets. The keeper of the pet store will tell you what foods to buy for the types of fish you own.

Health. If you suspect that one of your fish is sick, separate it from the others. Tiny white spots on its body may indicate ichthyophthirius, called ich for short. It is a common ailment. Your pet store has medicine to cure it.

If you notice a fish gulping at the surface, it probably isn't getting enough oxygen from the water. You may need a new air pump, or your tank may be overcrowded. Remember, without oxygen to breathe, fish drown!

Breeding. Saltwater fish rarely breed in captivity, but many freshwater species do. Many fish will breed only if their living conditions are excellent. Most fish lay eggs, but some, like *guppies,* bear live young. Other fish, like *bettas* and *gourami*, build bubble nests into which they insert their eggs. A betta male catches the female's eggs as she releases them and blows them into their foamy nests. Adult fish sometimes eat their own eggs and offspring. Aquarium plants give the small fry places to hide.

Choosing Fish. Before choosing fish, decide what kind of aquarium you want. There are four main kinds: (1) *cold-water freshwater;* (2) *tropical freshwater;* (3) *cold-water saltwater;* (4) *tropical saltwater.* Saltwater fish are more difficult to keep than freshwater varieties. Start with easy, inexpensive kinds. With experience, you'll be able to keep more costly tropical specimens. A keeper of a pet store can advise you about the kinds to choose. If you are buying more than one type, make sure they won't fight with each other. Remember, most big fish eat little fish.

Freshwater Fish. The choices are endless. *Barbs* are colorful and easy to keep. *Catfish* act somewhat like janitors (cleaning the tank's water by eating leftover food.) *Goldfish* are the most popular and easiest to keep (*See GOLD-FISH*). *Guppies* are the champion breeders among aquarium fish. One female can give birth to from eighteen to fifty young every month. *Kissing gourami* seem to kiss each other, but this mouth-to-mouth habit probably has nothing to do with love. *Mollies* are not only pretty, but helpful also. They devour leftovers and eat algae that grow on glass walls. Beware of *paradise fish* because they don't act angelic. The males frequently bite others. *Platy*, however, are peaceful. *Swordtails* have gorgeous tail fins and, like guppies, they bear live young. *Tetras* don't fight and they are very attractive. Striped *zebra danios* are a delight to behold.

   Tropical Fish. There are thousands of beautiful and interesting varieties that can be purchased at pet shops. *Angelfish*, *butterfly fish*, and *damselfish* are brilliantly colored. *Gobies* are unusual because they have sucking disks that enable them to stick to the sides of an aquarium. *Sea horses* have horselike heads and monkeylike tails. They shouldn't be kept with other kinds of fish because they can't compete at mealtimes and may starve while faster fish devour food. *Wrasses* are hide-and-seek pets that often bury themselves in the tank's bottom.

FOX TERRIERS. Fox terriers are originally from England, where they were used to hunt foxes. They are friendly, playful, and excel at learning tricks. Many are star performers in theatrical dog acts. *See also* DOGS.

FROGS AND TOADS. These are *amphibians*—animals that spend part of their lives in water and part of their lives on land. They are noisy creatures and can be heard calling to their mates on spring and summer evenings. Of the hundreds of kinds of frogs and toads, many varieties make good pets.

   Although frogs and toads are similar, they do have some differences. Frogs have smooth, slippery skin. Toads have rough, bumpy, dry skin. Toads are shorter and plumper than frogs, and they usually hop around. Frogs leap and jump.

   Housing. *Woodland frogs and toads* should have tanks with gravel, soil, moss, tree branches, a rock or two, bark to hide under, and a large, heavy bowl to soak in. *Tree frogs* need plenty of branches to climb on.

   Aquatic frogs need aquariums filled with several inches of water for swimming. Make an island of rocks, soil, or gravel for them to rest on. Tap water must be aged before it goes into the tank. Place the water in large jars and let it stand for two days so that all the chlorine evaporates. Replace the tank water when it becomes dirty.

Toad

Feeding. Frogs and toads eat insects and worms which they catch with quick flicks of their long, sticky tongues. Normally, they eat only live food, but in captivity they can learn to dine on dead flies and ground meat. Dangle food from a piece of thread or a pair of tweezers to make it seem alive. Frogs and toads ignore motionless food. Live mealworms, bought at pet stores, are healthy treats for your pet.

Feed your frog or toad several times a week. If it refuses to eat, return it to the wild where you found it. Some wild animals refuse to eat in captivity.

Handling. Hold a frog or toad gently in your hand. A large frog can be grasped just behind the forelegs. Will toads give you warts? Don't believe that superstition! However, most toads have poisonous mucus on their skins that protects them from hungry animals. Any animal that eats a toad can become sick and possibly die. Getting this mucus on your hands is harmless, but if you touch your eyes or mouth, they will burn. Always wash your hands after handling toads. *See also* TADPOLES.

G

GEESE. Domestic geese can be tame pets, but they are often very noisy. They act as "guard geese," honking and hissing at visitors. Geese don't usually chase people they know, but they may chase and nip at strangers.

Geese are sociable birds that like to live in family groups. Their wing feathers can be clipped by an expert to keep them from flying away. You can tame geese by giving them small amounts of grain every day.

Housing. Geese are very hardy birds. They don't need ponds for swimming, but they do need water for drinking and bathing. Geese also need shrubs or a shelter for shade and protection.

Feeding. Most of the year geese eat grass. Because they spend so much time grazing, they have sometimes been used to weed around gardens.

In winter, when the grass is covered with snow, supply geese with grain, greens, and stale bread. Be sure they always have a large bucket of clean, fresh drinking water.

GERBILS. Not long ago, gerbils (pronounced "jur-bils") were unusual pets, but because they are easy to raise, they have become quite popular. All the pet gerbils in the United States were originally bred from gerbils imported from the Gobi Desert of Mongolia. These rodents were first brought to the United States in 1954 to be used in research laboratories.

Gerbils have gray-brown coats, long furry tails, large, bright eyes, and strong hind legs. They sometimes leap around like miniature kangaroos. They can jump forward, backward, and sideways. They are gentle, curious, sociable, clean, and odorless. Gerbils are happiest living in pairs. Note: In some states, keeping gerbils is illegal because if any get loose, they can multiply and destroy farmers' crops. *See also* RODENTS.

Gerbil

GERMAN SHEPHERDS. Because they respond so well to training, German shepherds are used to herd sheep, aid police, guard people and property, and guide the blind. They can sniff out narcotics, locate lost persons, and find bombs. These large dogs are devoted companions and excellent watchdogs. They need room to run, and their thick coats need brushing every few days. *See also* DOGS.

GOATS. These belong in the country, where there is plenty of space to graze and exercise. They can become affectionate pets that come when called and follow you around. They can also be naughty rascals that eat flowers, devour newspapers, and dance on top of cars. If a door is left open, your friendly goat may walk in, feel at home, munch on magazines, and leave droppings all over the floor.

Female goats make better pets than males. Males tend to be larger and bolder and give off a strong odor. Female goats can be raised for milk. A good milking goat produces about one gallon of milk per day for about nine or ten months of the year. But she must be bred yearly, or she will stop producing milk. Goats must be milked two or three times a day.

Housing. Goats need clean, dry shelter. A three-sided shed facing south, or a stall in a barn or garage will do. The shelter should contain feed and water buckets, and a salt lick. Bed the shelter with straw or wood shavings. Remove the bedding when it is dirty, and put down a fresh layer.

Each goat needs about an acre of land for grazing and exercise. Keep your goat tethered, or in a fenced-in field. Never tie your pet to a tree, or it may eat the bark and kill the tree.

Feeding. Goat chow, which is a mixture of grains, hay, and grass, makes a good goat diet. Goats like a wide variety of foods and can be given all sorts of vegetables. It's not true that goats eat tin cans. The creatures will, however, eat the labels off the cans and lick the salty glue underneath.

Feed goats grain twice a day. During the warm months they can graze all day. Be sure that they always have fresh water and a salt lick.

Goat

Health. If your goat won't eat or has diarrhea, constipation, or coughs frequently, call your veterinarian.

Normal exercise usually keeps goats' hooves worn down, but if the hooves grow too long, they should be trimmed.

Note: Many communities don't allow goats or other farm animals in backyards. Before buying a goat, check local laws.

GOLDEN RETRIEVERS. Originally bred to hunt and retrieve waterfowl, golden retrievers today are popular pets and are widely used as guide dogs for blind people. They are friendly, even tempered, and obedient. Their naturally gentle nature makes them wonderful with children. *See also* DOGS.

GOLDFISH. These fish were first domesticated 1,000 years ago in China, where nobility kept them in stone basins. Over the years Chinese and Japanese fish breeders have developed many unusual kinds. There are goldfish with fan tails, fringed tails, flowing fins, bulging eyes, and bumpy heads. Not all of them are golden in color. They may have silver, purple, red, or black markings. Some goldfish are pure white; others are jet black.

Goldfish are excellent first fish because they are easy to care for. Keep them in freshwater aquariums or in outdoor ponds. If your pond freezes in the winter, make sure it is deep enough for your fish to live under the ice.

Indoors, goldfish never grow more than a few inches long, but outdoors they may become a foot long. Properly cared for, goldfish can live more than twenty years in captivity! Fancy varieties are harder to keep, and they require warmer temperatures than common goldfish. *See also* FISH.

Goldfish

GREAT DANES. Giants of the dog kingdom, Great Danes can be 3 feet (.92 m) high and weigh up to 150 pounds (67.95 kg). These dogs once guarded the castles of German princes and English kings. Although their immense size frightens many people, they are very gentle. *See also* DOGS.

GREYHOUNDS. Fastest of dogs and one of the oldest of breeds, they were kept by Egyptians 5,000 years ago. At one time greyhounds were bred and raised by English aristocrats, and it was illegal for a British commoner to own a greyhound. Today these dogs are raced for sport. They can run as fast as 37 m.p.h. (59.53 km/h). Greyhounds are intelligent and tend to be high-strung. *See also* DOGS.

Greyhound

GUINEA PIGS. Guinea pigs aren't pigs, and they don't come from Guinea! They are plump rodents that originally came from South America, where they were domesticated by the Inca Indians of Peru. The Incas raised them for food and kept them as pets.

European traders brought the first guinea pigs across the Atlantic from South America. These traders were called "guineamen" by English-speaking people, which probably accounts for the name "guinea pig." Although not related to pigs, guinea pigs grunt and whistle like pigs. Some people call guinea pigs *cavies,* their Peruvian name.

Guinea pigs are used in many scientific experiments.

Bred in a wide variety of colors, with both long and short hair, you'll find them to be cute, cuddly, and easy to care for.

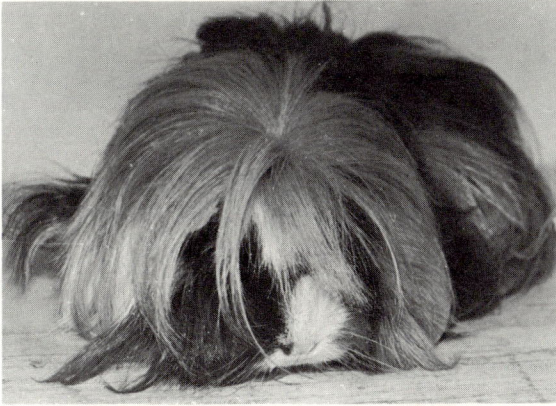

Long-haired guinea pig

Housing. Rabbit hutches make good guinea pig homes. The hutch should have shade and contain a covered box for sleeping and privacy. An upside-down shoebox with an entrance hole works well.

There should be a water bottle, a food dish, and materials for chewing inside the hutch. Use hay or wood shavings for bedding. Remove droppings every day. Replace bedding once a week.

In warm climates guinea pigs can live outside, but in cold areas they must live indoors. An outdoor hutch must be sturdily built up on high legs. This protects your pets from cats and dogs and keeps them off damp ground. Dampness and drafts can make them sick.

Because guinea pigs love to eat grass, it's a good idea to have a portable grazing run. A light wooden frame with wire on the sides and top works well. Cover part of the run with canvas or cloth to provide shade. Never leave your pet alone when it's in the portable run because it is defenseless against curious dogs and cats.

Feeding. Feed your pet guinea pig pellets, hay, lettuce, celery, and grass clippings that haven't been sprayed with insecticide. Fruits and vegetables, like apples, carrots, and potato peelings make healthy treats. During the day a dish of pellets should be left in the hutch. A salt block and fresh water must also be available.

Hungry guinea pigs will inform you of their desire to eat by honking, whistling, grunting, and squealing. Overweight in guinea pigs is usually the result of too little exercise rather than too much food. *See also* RODENTS.

H

HAMSTERS. All the pet hamsters in the world are descended from one male and three females that were captured in Syria in 1930. They were originally bred for scientific experiments, but because they are cute, clean, and easy to care for, they became popular pets.

The name *hamster* comes from the German verb *hamstern*, meaning to hoard or store away. Hamsters hoard food and have special pouches in their cheeks for carrying it. When filled, the pouches bulge out like little balloons.

Housing. Your hamster cage should be roomy enough to give your pet plenty of space to run and play. Use at least 2 inches (5.08 cm) of bedding and supply soft material for nesting. Install a water bottle, food dish, hard materials for gnawing, and toys, like ladders and exercise wheels.

Feeding. Hamsters eat hamster food (available at pet stores), fruits, and vegetables. Hamsters won't overeat—rapidly disappearing food is being hoarded, not eaten. Remove hoarded fruits and vegetables before they spoil. *See also* RODENTS.

HIMALAYAN CATS. These are a cross between Siamese and Persian cats. They combine the body structure and silky hair of Persians with the lovely two-toned markings of Siamese cats. *See also* CATS.

HORSES. These fine animals helped shape history. They carried knights into battle, plowed farmers' fields, moved heavy loads, and provided transporta-

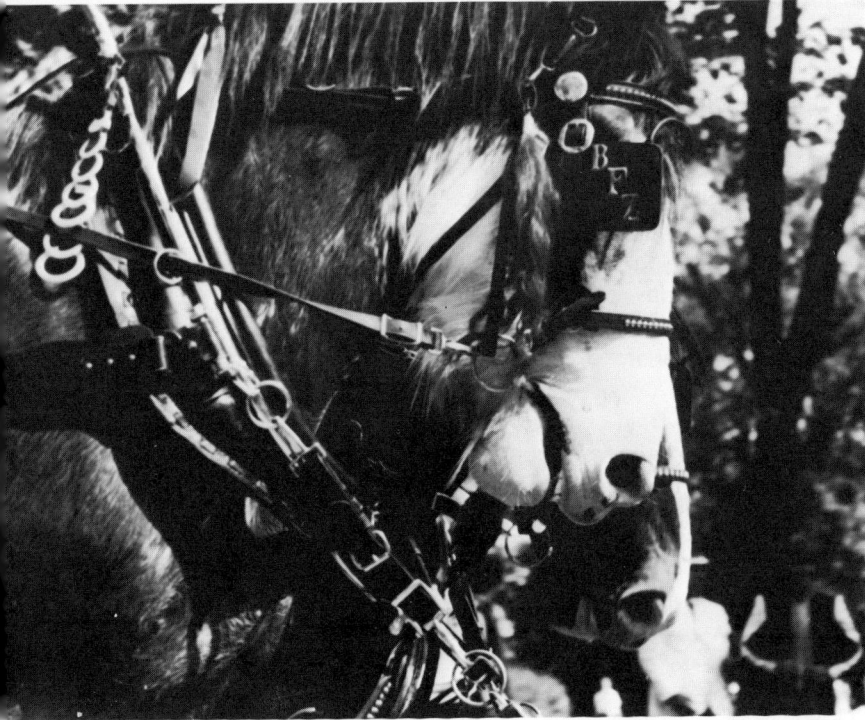

Work horses

tion. Today many horses are still used as work animals, but the majority of horses in North America are used for pleasure and sport.

Owning a horse is exciting and fun but requires a great deal of time, money, and work. Food, bedding, stable equipment, horseshoeing, and veterinary care must be paid for. And horses must be fed, groomed, exercised, and have their stalls cleaned every day.

It is important to know the basics of riding and horse care before you own a horse. Local 4-H clubs, pony clubs, and riding stables are good places to learn. If you decide to buy a horse, have an expert help you choose, and always have the animal examined by a vet. A horse's age, size, breed, sex, temperament, soundness, and degree of training must all be considered before investing in such a costly animal. Usually, older, well-trained horses make good first horses.

Housing. You can either board your horse at a stable, or, if you have at least two acres of land, you can keep it at home. Your horse can live in a barn or in a securely fenced-in pasture with a shed for protection against rain, wind, sun, and flies. Wooden fencing is recommended because horses can injure themselves on wire fences. Never use barbed wire.

If your horse lives in a barn, its stall should be 12 feet by 12 feet (3.66 m by 3.66 m), clean, airy, dry, and deeply bedded with straw or wood shavings. The stall must contain a water bucket, a feed trough, and a salt block. Cover all windows with strong inside screening.

Clean your horse's stall every day. Remove all manure and wet bedding. Add fresh bedding, and refill the water bucket at least once a day.

Feeding. Consult your veterinarian to decide what diet is best for your horse. Horses should be fed two or three meals a day, at the same times every day. Good quality hay and some grain should make up the bulk of your animal's diet. Hay should be leafy, greenish in color, and free from mold. Even horses that are in pasture all day need some hay and grain. Horses need a lot of water.

Riding horses

Never feed your horse grain just before or after a heavy workout, because this could make it ill. Never change the diet suddenly, but change it gradually over a period of several days.

Care. Daily grooming is important. It keeps your horse's skin and coat in good condition. If your horse lives outside, it will need brushing a few times a week. However, it should be brushed before and after every ride. Clean your horse's hooves every day. Dirt and stones can collect in cracks and cause lameness. Horses' hooves never stop growing. They must be trimmed and shod by a blacksmith every six weeks. If your horse isn't ridden much, shoes may not be necessary.

After riding, cool your horse by walking it before putting it back in the stall.

Health. Have your horse vaccinated against tetanus, encephalitis, and influenza every spring and dewormed four to six times a year. Buy worming medicines from a veterinarian. Don't neglect this. Even fat, shiny horses can be loaded with worms.

If your horse shows signs of lameness, call your vet immediately. When caught early, most lameness can be cured. Some signs of illness are: refusal to eat or drink, discharge from eyes and nose, excessive sweating, a temperature of more than 103°F (39°C)—100° F (37° C) is normal—frequent lying down, rolling, and groaning. *See also* PONIES.

I-K

INSECTS. Easy pets to keep, most insects are able to live in a jar containing soil, twigs, and leaves. Although they have short life spans, they are worthwhile pets because they are fascinating to watch. You can see ants build tunnels, praying mantises catch flies, and caterpillars turn into butterflies or moths. *See also* ANTS; CATERPILLARS; CRICKETS; and PRAYING MANTISES.

IRISH SETTERS. Their long, silky, red hair makes Irish setters beautiful pets! They are country dogs and need lots of exercise and room to run. Be sure to

Irish setter

have identification tags on their collars because they tend to wander. Although some setters are high-strung, they are extremely gentle with children. *See also* DOGS.

KORAT CATS. These beautiful creatures have coats of glossy, silver blue or silvery, slate gray. In Thailand, Korat cats are symbols of good luck. They were first imported into the United States in the 1930s. *See also* CATS.

Korat cat

L

LABRADOR RETRIEVERS. Labradors are popular hunting dogs and guide dogs for the blind. Because they are friendly, gentle, and loyal, Labrador Retrievers make excellent pets. Their short, dense coats provide protection from cold weather and icy water. *See also* DOGS.

LHASA APSOS. These are small, active dogs that were developed in Tibet centuries ago. They are very intelligent and can be easilv trained. Their long, straight coats need regular combing. Because Lhasa apsos can be quick tempered, they aren't suitable around young children. *See also* DOGS.

Lhasa apso

LIZARDS. Scaly reptiles that look like miniature dragons, lizards are found in most parts of the world and are common in warm climates. There are approximately 3,000 kinds. Some are as long as a human finger; others are as long as a bed. The largest, the Komodo Dragon of Southeast Asia, is 10 feet (3.05 m) long.

Only little lizards make suitable pets. They are usually clean, odorless, and lively. Like snakes, they shed their skins periodically. The skin usually comes off in patches rather than in one piece.

Anoles: The anole (pronounced a-no-lee) is the most popular of pet lizards. Carolina anoles are sometimes mistakenly called chameleons (see entry below) because they change colors when light, temperature, or their emotional mood changes. For example, a brown anole can turn bright green when frightened.

Special toe pads enable these creatures to climb walls and walk on ceilings. A male anole has an orange or red throat sac which he blows up like a balloon whenever he is ready to fight or mate. Don't keep two males in the same cage because they may fight.

Chameleons: Chameleons are odd-looking lizards from Africa and south Asia with narrow bodies, bulging eyes, and very long, sticky tongues for catching insects. Chameleons can change colors, and they are interesting to watch, but since they rarely live for more than a year in captivity, they aren't suitable pets.

Geckos: Geckos are tropical lizards that hunt insects at night. (Like anoles, they scamper up walls and walk on ceilings.) Because they are active at night and many of them bite, they aren't good pets.

Iguanas: Some people manage to enjoy having an iguana as a pet. However, because this odd-looking lizard can grow to 6 feet (1.82 m) long, only someone with plenty of space and permission from all members of the family should consider keeping an iguana. Sharp teeth and claws make it hard to handle.

Housing. Lizard cages should be roomy, easy to clean, and kept at a constant temperature of 72° to 85° F (22° to 29° C). Equip the cage with branches for climbing, rocks, tree bark for shelter, a large water dish, and a thermometer. Check the cage's temperature daily so that your pet isn't baked or chilled.

Cover the floor of the cage with sand or newspaper. Clean the cage whenever it becomes dirty, and remove food that isn't eaten. Place the cage in a sunny spot, or heat it with a lamp. Shade must always be available so that your lizard can cool off when it gets too hot. Cover your cage with a securely fitted top made of screen wire, pegboard, or plywood that has air holes.

Feeding. Insects or canned dog food supplemented with fresh greens are suitable for most pet lizards. Many of them won't drink water from a dish, so sprinkle the plants in the cage with water every day. Feed your lizards two to three times a week.

Handling. Never lift a lizard by its tail because it may snap off! You'll be left holding a tail while the rest of the animal escapes. Most lizards lose their tails when cornered by enemies. A new tail grows, but it is shorter and stumpier than the original.

LOVEBIRDS. Originally from Africa, these small members of the parrot family love living in pairs. They earned their name because they groom, feed, and act lovingly toward each other. Their beautiful colors and delightful ways make them desirable pets. However, lovebirds sometimes chirp noisily and, therefore, may not be appreciated in a small apartment. Like their relatives, cockatiels, and parakeets, they eat seeds, fresh vegetables, and fresh fruits. *See also* BIRDS and PARROTS.

M-N

MAINE COON CATS. Early New Englanders believed that Maine coon cats were a cross between raccoons and cats. However, raccoons and cats can't produce offspring because they do not belong to the same species. Experts now believe that coon cats descended from local tabby-striped cats and long-haired cats brought to New England by sailors.

Maine coon cats are prized by New Englanders for their size and beauty. *See also* CATS.

MANX CATS. Cats with long hind legs and no tails! They hop around like rabbits. Manx cats have been bred for centuries off the west coast of England on the Isle of Man.

Completely tailless Manx are called *rumpies,* while those with short stumps are called *stumpies.* They come in a variety of colors. Only the tailless ones are allowed to compete in cat shows. *See also* CATS.

MICE. About ten thousand years ago, when people began storing grain, mice moved into houses and barns. They have stayed with us ever since. Mice have been hunted as pests, used in scientific experiments, and taken into homes as pets.

A mouse may weigh only an ounce (31.10 g) and fit into the palm of your hand. Although shy and timid, a mouse can become tame with gentle handling.

There are white, yellow, red, brown, black, gray, and spotted mice. They may be long-haired, short-haired, or even hairless. One variety, the *waltzing mouse,* dances in circles. An inner ear defect upsets its sense of balance and causes it to spin around.

Housing. Because a mouse can squeeze through a hole that is less than half an inch wide (15.24 cm), cages should be glass, plastic, or closely woven wire mesh. Mice are entertaining acrobats and enjoy ladders, shelves, wheels, trapezes, and exercise bars. This equipment keeps them busy and observers amused. Bedding can be sawdust or wood shavings. Material like cotton, soft paper, or pieces of wool should be provided for sleeping nests. A small box inside the cage makes a dollhouse-size bedroom fit for a mouse. Mice are clean creatures. They lick and wash themselves like cats and usually use the corner farthest from their nest as their bathroom. Pile the bedding high in this corner, and remove the soiled bedding every day. If you don't, there will be an unpleasant ''mouse smell.'' Every week or two clean the entire cage, washing it with soap and hot water. When the cage dries, rebed it for your pets.

Feeding. Have food available at all times for these champion nibblers. They eat just about anything. A balanced diet consists of seeds, grains, and fresh vegetables. Give your mouse hard-shelled nuts, bones, and twigs to chew on, and, of course, a supply of fresh, clean water. Cheese is *not* their favorite food, and it isn't the ideal meal for them. *See also* RODENTS.

MYNA BIRDS. Mynas are talkers that can learn to say words and phrases so clearly that they sound human. The mynas most commonly found in pet stores are *Indian Hill mynas* that originally came from southeast Asia and India. They are glossy black birds with bright yellow beaks and yellow eye markings.

Because they are large, myna birds need large cages and plenty of exercise outside their cages. Give them pet-store myna food and fresh fruit, like apples, bananas, peaches, and plums. Live mealworms make good weekly snacks. Myna birds drink lots of water and like to bathe frequently. Their droppings are messy, and their cages need daily cleaning. *See also* BIRDS.

NEWFOUNDLANDS. These huge, powerful dogs have been used to rescue thousands of drowning people. In the 1800s many ships carried Newfoundlands that were trained to jump overboard and rescue people. Their thick, dark coats protect them from icy waters. Although these dogs are large and strong, they have gentle natures and make wonderful pets. *See also* DOGS.

P

PARAKEETS. These small, colorful members of the parrot family are among the most popular pets. Both males and females chatter and sing.

Budgerigars are the most common parakeet pets. Originally from Australia, they are colorful, lively, and playful. Some can be trained to say words, phrases, and even recite poems!

Parakeets are happier when kept in pairs. They seem to thrive on affection, and they enjoy toys like ladders, ropes, and seed bells. Like other small parrots, they eat seeds, fresh fruits and vegetables and need cuttlebone and grit. *See also* BIRDS.

PARROTS. Because they are able to "talk" and to mimic all sorts of sounds, parrots have become prized pets. They whistle tunes, sing songs, laugh, sneeze, and sound out words and sentences.

Most parrots in the United States are imported from South America. Expensive and not easy to keep, these large birds need big strong cages and plenty of exercise. Some tame ones can live on perches outside cages. These birds usually have their wings clipped so that they can't fly away.

A parrot can be a long-time investment. Healthy ones live from fifteen to eighty years. Therefore, be sure you are willing to take the responsibility of caring for one. Zoos frequently receive calls from people who no longer want their pet parrots.

Parrot

Parrots can be noisy and messy. Unless they are trained properly, their strong beaks and large claws can hurt you. When they do become tame, "Pollies" grow very attached to their owners and are very affectionate.

Parrots eat seeds, fruits, nuts, and fresh greens. Like other birds, they need sand or grit to aid digestion and twigs or blocks of wood to chew on. Give your parrot a large pan of water to bathe in, or spray your pet with a mister.

African Grays are considered the best talkers. They are a lovely soft gray with bright red tails and black bills. African Grays can learn to say close to a thousand words.

Amazons are the most popular of the South American parrots. They can become good talkers. However, they are expensive and need lots of living space.

Cockatiels are relatively large (about 12 inches—365.76 cm) with crested heads, long tails, and graceful wings. Because they are peaceful and gentle, cockatiels can be kept with finches and other small birds.

Cockatoos are large white birds with crested heads. They come from Pacific islands. Although beautiful, they shriek and aren't suitable in small apartments or in homes where people enjoy quiet.

Macaws are the largest and most expensive parrots. These brilliantly colored birds come from South America's rain forests, where they can be heard screaming to each other high in the treetops.

Noisy and destructive, macaws can easily chew up electrical wires and pull wooden furniture to bits with their strong beaks and claws. They must be handled with caution.

Because they command a high price, many macaws are illegally smuggled out of their native countries. They frequently become ill and die from mistreatment. Unfortunately, their population is rapidly decreasing. *See also* BIRDS.

PEKINGESE DOGS. The tiny, long-haired Pekingese dog was held sacred and kept in palaces by Chinese emperors. For centuries its breeding was carefully guarded by the court, and the punishment for stealing one of them was death! The first Pekingese to reach England were stolen from the Imperial Palace in Peking in 1860.

Pekingese don't need much exercise, but they require daily brushing to keep their long, smooth coats looking good. Because Pekingese can be high-strung, they aren't suitable pets for children. *See also* DOGS.

PERSIAN CATS. Well known for their long, silky coats, their beauty and good dispositions combine to make them the most popular long-haired cats in the United States. There are numerous color varieties. All have stocky builds with large, round heads. *See also* CATS.

Bi-color Persian cat

PIGEONS. Pet pigeons are not the wild varieties we see perched on park statues and pecking away at food on city streets. The pigeons you purchase in pet stores and from breeders are specially bred for their beauty or flying ability. There are over three hundred breeds in assorted sizes, shapes, and colors.

Flying pigeons are also known as *homing pigeons* and *carrier pigeons*. At one time they provided the world's first airmail service. Before the invention of the telegraph and telephone, these birds carried messages to battle stations and to government leaders. Then the pigeons returned home, often traveling thousands of miles.

All pigeons have an instinct that enables them to find their way home. Today, specially trained "flyers" race back to their roosts from distances as far as 600 miles (965.4 km) away. Pigeon racing is popular, and special clubs arrange competitions. In Belgium it is a national sport.

Certain flyers are bred for their unusual acrobatics. A group known as *tumblers* turn backward somersaults as they fly. *Parlor tumblers* perform somersaults on the ground. *Rollers* roll and spin in the air.

Fancy pigeons come in a wide variety of colors and shapes. *Fantails* remind one of miniature peacocks; *fairy swallows* wear feathered "slippers" on their feet, and *pouters* blow their crops (throats) up like balloons.

Pigeons are usually sold in pairs. Because young birds are easier to train, it's best to buy them when they are less than a year old. Choose birds that are active and have smooth, clean feathers. There is no scientific difference between pigeons and doves. Smaller, more delicate pigeons are usually called doves.

Housing. Pigeons need clean, uncrowded living conditions. Their homes are called *lofts* or *pens*. These should have solid, weatherproof roofs, wood and poultry-wire walls, and wood or concrete floors.

The loft or pen should be equipped with nesting boxes containing hay, straw, pine needles or burlap, perches, feeding troughs, and water dishes. A big shallow pan about 5 inches (152.4 cm) deep should be provided daily for bathing. Remove the bathwater after a few hours so that the birds don't drink from it.

Cover the flooring with sand. Rake off the droppings and sprinkle fresh sand each week. Clean the entire cage periodically.

Flying pigeons sometimes live in lofts built on posts or attached to trees or roofs of barns, sheds, or garages. Fancy pigeons can live in smaller pens, but be sure they have enough room for exercise.

Feeding. Commercial pigeon food makes an excellent basic diet. It is a mixture of dried peas, beans, corn, and other grains. Place pigeon food in a feed trough large enough so that all birds can eat at the same time. Feed them two meals a day—one in the morning and one in the late afternoon. Offer greens, like lettuce, celery tops, or grass clippings, about once a week. Allow them to eat as much as they like for about fifteen to twenty minutes; then remove the rest.

Like other birds, pigeons have no teeth. They eat grit to grind their food. Specially prepared mixtures of grit, minerals, and salt (bought at feed stores) should always be available for your birds. Always have a clean, fresh supply of water for your pigeons.

POINTERS. Popular hunting dogs and gentle pets, pointers stop and "freeze," pointing their noses in the direction of game while hunting. They hold this pose until their master shoots the game. Pointers are active, enjoyable pets. They are country dogs and need lots of exercise and room to run. *See also* DOGS.

PONIES. Horses that are less than 58 inches (147 cm) at the withers (base of the neck) when fully grown are called ponies. Their care is very similar to that of horses, but many small ponies don't need shoes, and, of course, they eat less than their larger cousins. *See also* HORSES.

POODLES. The most popular dog breed in the United States, poodles come in three different size varieties: *toy, miniature,* and *standard.* Because they are exceptionally smart, poodles can easily learn tricks. They are star performers in many circuses where they jump high hurdles, turn somersaults, skip rope, and dance.

At one time poodles were hunting dogs used to retrieve waterfowl. Their owners clipped their heavy coats to make swimming easier. Today most poodles are clipped to keep their thick curly hair manageable—and fashionable. *See also* DOGS.

PRAYING MANTISES. The praying mantis received its name because it folds its front legs and raises them as though in prayer. The mantis holds this saintly pose until its goggle-eyes see another insect. Then its strong, spiked legs grab the victim.

These odd-looking insects make useful pets. They can roam about the house and clear it of other insects. After eating, they wash their faces and feet just like cats. When they become used to you, they take food from your fingers.

Mantis egg cases can be bought by mail or in some garden supply stores. Gardeners and farmers buy praying mantises because they kill insects that feed on flowers and crops. Mantises are considered so valuable for this purpose that, in many states, killing them is illegal.

Housing. The egg cases must be kept outdoors over the winter, then brought inside in early spring and placed inside a jar covered with cheesecloth. Over one hundred tiny praying mantises will emerge sometime in the spring. The babies must be separated or released outdoors, or they will eat each other.

An adult praying mantis can live in a jar covered with cheesecloth or screening. Supply your pet with a few twigs to perch on.

Feeding. Your mantis will need several insects to eat every day. Almost any insects that are alive and moving will be gobbled up quickly by your ever-hungry pet. Spray the jar with water daily to give your pet drinking water. *See also* INSECTS.

R

RABBITS. Domestically raised rabbits are the only rabbits that make good pets. Wild rabbits are easy to handle when young, but when they become older they may kick and bite, or carry a contagious disease.

Breeders and pet stores sell tame rabbits. Many of these creatures are affectionate, and some can even be house-trained. Over sixty breeds of rabbit have been developed—all descendants of wild European rabbits. They are of many colors and shapes. Some weigh only 2 to 3 pounds (.90 to 1.36 kg); others weigh more than 20 pounds (9 kg). One breed, the *lop*, has long, droopy ears that may be more than 2 feet (6 m long)!

Housing. Most rabbits can live all year in outdoor pens, called *hutches*. A typical hutch has a completely sheltered sleeping box (bedded with straw, hay, or wood shavings) and an open-air wire-mesh run for fresh air and exercise. Wire floors enable the droppings to fall through to the ground. Some rabbits, however, get sore feet from standing on wire. A wood floor covered with hay, straw, or wood shavings may be more comfortable for your pet.

An outdoor hutch should be raised on legs to protect your pet against dampness and curious animals, like cats and dogs. It should have a sloping, weathertight roof. A hutch 2 feet (.61 m) wide, 4 feet (1.22 m) long, and 2 feet (.61 m) high is good for an average-size rabbit. Of course, the roomier, the better. With the exception of a mother and her babies, each rabbit should have its own hutch. Occasionally two friendly females can bunk together, but males will fight.

Albino rabbit

Keep your rabbit's hutch clean and dry. Remove droppings and stale food daily. Give the hutch a thorough cleaning once a week. Remove all bedding, wash the hutch with soap and warm water, rinse well, and supply new bedding after the hutch is dry.

It is possible to train a rabbit to live inside your home. Housebreaking isn't difficult because rabbits always use the same spot for their droppings. Place a shallow box with cat litter in your rabbit's favorite bathroom corner.

Although you may enjoy your bunny as a house pet during the day, it is wise to put it to bed in a hutch at night. Otherwise, your pet may chew your furniture and electrical wires while you sleep.

Portable hutches or exercise pens allow your rabbit to exercise and eat fresh grass. These hutches have no bottoms and can be moved from place to place. Keep an eye on your pet when it is grazing in its portable hutch. Make sure it doesn't escape and is safe from other animals.

Feeding. Buy rabbit pellets and add fresh foods like carrots, lettuce, cabbage, and clover. Wash all fresh food carefully, and never offer greens that have been treated with insecticides.

Rabbits tend to overeat. Too many fresh foods can give them diarrhea. A breeder or pet-store manager can help you determine just how much to feed your pet.

Rabbits should be fed once a day, preferably in the afternoon, since they are active at night. Never dump food on the floor; use a dish. Remove uneaten greens every morning. Place a salt block, fresh water, and twigs or hardwood for chewing inside the hutch.

Handling and Grooming. *Never lift a rabbit by its ears.* Rabbits' ears are very delicate and can be injured easily. Lift your bunny by the loose skin on the back of its neck, and support its body with your other hand. Be gentle! If handled roughly, a rabbit may scratch, kick, and bite.

Most rabbits keep themselves well-groomed by licking themselves. However, long-haired rabbits need to be combed and brushed. Brush gently, for rabbits have tender skin and fine hair. If your pet's nails grow too long, your veterinarian can clip them.

Health. Common signs of illness are loss of appetite, runny nose, dull eyes, rough coat, and prolonged diarrhea.

RATS. Most wild rats are large, dirty, and vicious. They can chew through lead pipes and concrete, and they cause billions of dollars of damage each year. But rats sold in pet stores are clean, friendly, and easy to tame. They are smarter, calmer, and more sociable than most other rodents. Pet rats are descendants of an albino strain of Norway rats.

Housing. Rats need roomy cages with toys, such as ladders and wheels, a water bottle, a feed dish, and a nesting box. Cover the cage floor with several inches of wood shavings, hay, or commercially bought bedding. Remove droppings every day, and change bedding at least once a month. If fleas are a problem, spray the cage with flea spray made for cats. Never use flea spray made for dogs because it is too strong for rodents.

Rats can be let loose to play in your room. They rarely try to escape, and they love to play. However, keep a close watch. You don't want them to trim their teeth on your furniture.

Rats and mice should never be kept together. Although they are close relatives, they are natural enemies.

Feeding. Rats eat just about anything, but it is important to give your pets a well-balanced diet. Feed them rat pellets (sold in pet stores), seeds, grains, and fresh vegetables. An occasional treat of mealworms, or whole wheat bread soaked in milk, is a healthy addition.

Rats' teeth may grow as much as 6 inches (15.24 cm) in three years if they don't chew hard objects. Supply bones, twigs, hard-shelled nuts, or blocks of wood—all perfect for gnawing. *See also* RODENTS.

REPTILES. These first appeared on the earth about 300 million years ago. About 6,000 kinds are scattered throughout the earth, but most of them live in the tropics. Reptiles have tough, waterproof skin that keeps them from drying out in the hot sun.

Different kinds of lizards, snakes, and turtles make interesting pets. Alligators and crocodiles become too large and dangerous to be pets, and poisonous reptiles should never be kept. *See also* LIZARDS; SNAKES; and TURTLES.

Anole reptile

Cornish rex cat

REX CATS. Rex are odd-looking cats with short, tightly curled hair. Rex come in many different colors. They are affectionate pets. Because their short, soft coats don't shed, they are good pets for people with allergies. *See also* CATS.

RODENTS. The idea of owning a rodent may not sound appealing, but these small, furry creatures make wonderful pets. They are inexpensive, easy to care for, interesting to watch, and fun to play with.

Rodents are mammals with sharp, chisellike front teeth that are perfect for gnawing. Many wild rodents, like mice and rats, are considered pests. They invade houses and other buildings, eating whatever they can and gnawing their way through all sorts of objects, even lead pipes.

Gerbils, guinea pigs, and hamsters were originally brought into the United States from foreign countries to be used in laboratories. Scientists have discovered that these pesky creatures make valuable subjects for scientific experiments. By using rodents, important discoveries about food, drugs, genetics, and disease have been made in laboratories all over the world. Because they are cute and easy to care for, these useful laboratory animals have become very popular house pets.

Housing. The common rodent pets—gerbils, guinea pigs, hamsters, mice, and rats—can live in cages inside your home. The cage should be large enough for them to run in and must be made of metal, hard plastic, or wood lined with wire mesh. These materials prevent your pets from chewing their way to freedom. A glass aquarium with a wire-mesh top will do for mice and gerbils.

Rodents' teeth never stop growing, and by gnawing on objects these animals keep their teeth trimmed. If they don't have anything to chew, their teeth grow too long. Provide pieces of unpainted hardwood, twigs, and dog biscuits.

Keep the cage away from dampness, drafts, and bright sunlight. A temperature between 70° and 80° F (21° and 26° C) is ideal.

Cover the bottom with woodshavings, hay, or commercial bedding (bought at pet stores). Furnish the cage with soft material (like cloth or paper towels) for nesting, a sleeping box, a food dish, water bottle, and toys, like ladders, shelves, and exercise wheels. Give the cage a light cleaning every day and a thorough cleaning every week.

Feeding. Prepared food mixtures or pellets from your pet shop, plus fresh fruits, vegetables, and nuts make a good diet. Give your pet treats from your hand to help tame it, but make sure you handle your friend gently. Fresh, clean water must always be available. *See also* GERBILS; GUINEA PIGS; HAMSTERS; MICE; and RATS.

RUSSIAN BLUE CATS. Russian blues have short, thick, silky-fine hair that resembles seal skin. They are graceful and noble and have gentle dispositions. *See also* CATS.

S

SAINT BERNARDS. These large, powerful dogs were originally bred by monks in the Swiss Alps for rescue and guide work. They fearlessly brave snow and ice to find people lost in storms or buried in avalanches and safely guide travelers over snow-covered trails. These massive dogs are friendly, gentle, and good with children. They make sweet-natured pets. *See also* DOGS.

Saint Bernard and clumber spaniel

SALAMANDERS. These creatures resemble lizards, but their skins lack scales, and they don't have claws. Lizards are reptiles. Salamanders are amphibians.

Most salamanders are a few inches long. There are, however, giant salamanders in Japan that reach a length of over 5 feet (1.52 m).

Some salamanders live in water, some on land, and others in burrows and caves. They can be found under wet leaves, rocks, and rotting logs. Before handling one of these creatures, be sure to wet your hands so you don't injure its skin. Place wet leaves in your collecting container, and be sure your container has air holes.

When frightened, a salamander may shed its tail, but it eventually grows a new one. It can also grow a new leg after one is lost in a fight or an accident.

It's possible to raise your own pet salamanders from the jellylike egg masses found in ponds and brooks. These eggs and the newly hatched salamanders can be raised the same way you raise tadpoles. *See also* TADPOLES.

A *newt* is a type of salamander that has a flattened tail. Many are brightly colored. Newts make good pets.

Housing. Salamanders need moisture. Never place them in direct sunlight because their skins may dry up and they'll die. Make sure you know what kind of salamander you have so you can provide the right kind of home.

Salamanders that live in water should be housed in *aquatic terraria*—tanks filled with water, floating plants, and rocks. The water must be aged by letting it stand in jars for two days. This allows chlorine to evaporate. Change the water whenever it becomes cloudy or dirty.

Land-living salamanders need *woodland terraria*—glass tanks with soil, moss, plants, and tree bark for shelter. Keep the plants moist by spraying them with water. Provide a swimming hole filled with clean, aged water. Change the water in the swimming hole every day.

Salamanders that live both on land and in water need semi*aquatic terraria*—tanks that are half water and half land, with soil, plants, and bark. Cover your terrarium with a weighted screen lid to prevent escapes.

Feeding. Insects, worms, slugs, and snails can be eaten by salamanders. They normally eat only living food but can be taught to eat small pieces of meat, fish, and canned dog food. Because salamanders ignore food that doesn't move, dangle the "dead" food from a thread or tweezers to make it seem alive. Feed them every day. *See also* AMPHIBIANS.

SCHNAUZERS. There are three types of schnauzers—giant, standard, and miniature. All three have wiry coats and bristling eyebrows and whiskers. They are sturdy, intelligent, good guards, and make fine family pets. *See also* DOGS.

SCOTTISH TERRIERS. ''Scotties'' are very strong for their small size. At one time they were used to hunt small animals, but today they are raised primarily as family pets. *See also* DOGS.

SHETLAND SHEEPDOGS. Affectionately known as ''shelties,'' these dogs look like miniature collies. They were originally bred to tend sheep on the Shetland Islands off Scotland. Today shelties are raised as farm dogs and pets. Some Shetland sheepdogs are timid and high-strung, but because they are bright, sensitive, and intelligent, they make excellent pets. *See also* DOGS.

SHIH TZUS. This gem of an import from China, but native to Tibet originally, is a tiny, long-haired beauty whose face is a mass of hanging hairs that grow in all directions. Once a favorite of Ming Dynasty emperors, Shih Tzus have become very popular dogs, delighting owners all over the world. *See also* DOGS.

Shih Tzu

SIAMESE CATS. In ancient Siam, Siamese cats were bred by temple monks and owned by priests and aristocrats. Today they are one of the most popular breeds. These long, slim, elegant cats with two-toned coloring are often cross-eyed or kinky-tailed. They have strong, distinctive personalities, are playful, and demand lots of attention.

Siamese cats are sociable and intelligent animals, but some people find them noisy and high-strung. *See also* CATS.

SIBERIAN HUSKIES. These handsome dogs were brought from Siberia to Alaska in 1909 for sled-dog races. Their grace and speed made them winners in contests and very popular. Huskies are good guards and friendly companions. They require lots of exercise and grooming. *See also* DOGS.

SNAKES. Although many people are afraid of snakes, most of these animals are not only harmless, they are helpful. Snakes kill rats and other rodents that destroy crops and invade homes. They make fascinating pets. Snakes are quiet, odorless, easy to keep, and fun to watch.

It's usually best to acquire a pet snake from a pet store. Young snakes are easiest to tame, and it is fun to watch them grow.

Housing. Snakes should be housed in large glass cages that have securely fitted mesh-screen lids. Since snakes are talented escape artists, be sure that the lid has a good latch. The cage should be at least as long as the snake—the larger, the better.

Cover the bottom of the cage with newspapers or wood shavings. Fortunately, snakes are clean creatures, so their cages don't need daily cleaning.

Equip the cage with a sturdy water dish that is large enough for the snake to bathe in, branches and rocks, and a box for shelter. Keep a thermometer inside the cage so that you can check the air temperature. Snakes are cold-blooded, and their bodies become the same temperature as the air. Their homes must never be too hot or cold. (In the wild, snakes hibernate when the warm weather ends.)

Feeding. A snake has loosely attached jaws that unhinge and open wide and can eat an animal that is several times larger than its own head. Snakes don't chew their food, they swallow it whole. Don't keep a snake if you're squeamish. You must feed it live food like worms, mice, and frogs. You can obtain these at pet stores, or you can hunt for them or raise your own. Some snakes learn to accept raw fish and meats. Adult snakes don't eat often. Some eat once a week; others go for weeks without eating. Small snakes eat more often than large ones.

If your snake is offered a live meal, such as a mouse, and doesn't devour it soon, remove the mouse, or it may bite your snake. If two snakes are living in the same cage, make sure they don't grab the same piece of food, because the smaller snake may be swallowed along with the intended meal!

Some wild snakes will not eat in captivity. If this happens, turn the snake loose where you found it.

Handling. Pick up your snake just below the head, and support its body with your other arm. Don't squeeze a snake, for you might fracture its delicate ribs.

Choosing a Snake. Snakes can be as small as earthworms or longer than buses. It's easiest to keep those that are less than 4 feet (1.22 m) long. *Poisonous snakes should never be kept as pets.* If you plan to catch a wild snake, make absolutely sure you know what kind it is. Some snakes bite, and some are poisonous. There are excellent books that help you identify reptiles. Staff members at museums and parks can advise you.

Believe it or not, *boa constrictors* are popular pets. These beautifully patterned snakes from Central and South America kill small animals by squeezing them. In the wild they average 6 to 9 feet (1.83 to 2.74 m), and some grow to a length of 14 feet (4.27 m). These sizes are too large to be manageable—but there are pet owners who do manage *brown snakes*, *northern brown snakes* (also called *De Kay's snakes*), and *corn snakes*, all found in the wild. *Garter snakes* are the most common snakes in the United States, and they are the most popular of serpent pets. Garters are often found near water, where they hunt frogs, toads, and small fish.

King snakes respond well to handling, but they must live alone because they eat other snakes. Many kinds of *rat snakes* make good pets, but they grow to be between 3 and 6 feet (.91 and 1.83 m) long.

SPIDERS. There are over 40,000 kinds of spiders. Only a few are dangerous. The rest are not only harmless, they are helpful, because they kill large numbers of insects. Some spiders, like house spiders, garden spiders, wolf spiders, and tarantulas make interesting pets.

Housing. Keep your eight-legged pet in a jar or glass tank covered with screening. Keep only one spider in a container because spiders often eat each other. Furnish your spider's home with soil or gravel, twigs, leaves, and a rock or piece of bark for shelter. Sprinkle the cage with water every few days.

Not all spiders spin webs, but if yours does, make sure it has enough room. Spiders use their webs to trap insects, line their nests, incubate their eggs, and to wrap insects to preserve them for future dinners.

Periodically spiders shed their skins. While this happens, they may change color and remain inactive for several days. Don't disturb your spider during this time.

Feeding. Feed your spider whatever insects you can catch. Mealworms bought at pet stores also make good spider food. Some spiders can learn to eat from your hand.

Put a piece of sponge in a small dish to supply drinking water. Spiders drink by brushing their mouthparts with water. *See also* TARANTULAS.

Black and yellow garden spider

T

TADPOLES. Most frogs and toads begin their lives in water as tadpoles. Tadpoles, also called "pollywogs", look like tiny, wiggly fish. The change from tadpole to frog or toad is fascinating to watch.

Frogs' and toads' eggs can be found in pond and lake water in the springtime. Frog eggs are laid in jellylike clumps; toad eggs are laid in long strings. The eggs hatch within two weeks.

Place the eggs in an aquarium filled with pond water. Every few days replace some of the water with fresh pond water. Tadpoles need bits of algae and water plants to eat. They can also be given small pieces of lettuce and bits of worms.

Eventually tadpoles' tails will shrink and legs begin to grow. When the forelegs appear, the tadpoles will have developed lungs and will need to breathe air. Therefore, provide a rock island or sand ramp for them to climb onto.

After your tadpoles have turned into adult frogs and toads, you may want to keep one or two. Release the rest at the place where you found them. *See also:* FROGS AND TOADS.

TARANTULAS. Eight hairy legs, beady eyes, a fat body 3 inches (7.62 cm) long, and a leg span that may be 8 inches (20.32 cm)! Tarantulas look like nightmare monsters. People used to believe that their bite meant sudden death. Actually, though a bite can be painful, it is usually harmless. And tarantulas seldom bite, even when they are handled.

A tarantula should be housed in a glass tank with gravel on the floor and a rock for it to hide under. When the temperature drops below 60°F (15°C) use a heat lamp.

Tarantulas can survive without eating or drinking for more than a month. Feed your pet spider insects and mealworms, and supply a shallow dish for water. *See also:* SPIDERS.

TURTLES. These creatures crawled the earth and swam the seas 200 million years ago, when dinosaurs roamed our world. Their unique armored shells helped them survive through the ages. There are hundreds of kinds of turtles, ranging in size from a few inches to 7 feet (2.13 m). Some weigh an ounce (28.35 g), while others are as heavy as a horse.

There are three major groups of turtles: *land turtles* (tortoises); *freshwater turtles* (terrapins); and *marine turtles*. Marine turtles aren't suitable as pets because they require huge aquariums, but many land and freshwater turtles can be adopted and cared for easily.

Turtle

Perhaps you'll find a turtle in the woods or in a pond or stream. They are easy to catch because they are slow-moving, and it's simple to grab them by their shells. Turtles can scratch and bite, so be careful.

Snapping turtles don't make good pets. Their bites can cause serious injuries. Snappers have large heads, long necks, powerful jaws, and jagged shells.

Check the conservation laws in your area. In some states keeping any kind of turtle as a pet is illegal.

With a well-balanced diet, a clean, well-designed home, and proper care, a pet turtle can live for a long time. Some families have kept their shelled friends for twenty years.

Housing. Turtles can be kept in indoor tanks or in outdoor pens. Inside or outside, all turtles need both sunshine and shade. Because they are cold-blooded, their blood will heat up if they remain in the sun too long. They can die from heat, cold, and from sudden changes in temperature. Most water turtles need a temperature of 70° to 80° F (21° to 26°C). Land turtles do best at 75° to 85° F (23° to 28° C). Some tropical species need heating lamps to keep their homes properly heated. A thermometer enables you to check the temperature daily.

Land turtles can live in glass tanks with gravel floors indoors, or in securely enclosed outdoor pens. There should be a water basin big enough for your pet to swim in and tree bark or a box for shade and shelter.

Water turtles can live in outdoor pens like those for land turtles, but they need larger swimming pools. If you house your water turtle indoors, you will need a water-filled tank with dry gravel or rock islands, so that your pet can come ashore to sunbathe. Use water that has been standing for two days. This causes the chlorine in the water to evaporate. Change the water when it becomes cloudy, and clean the tank once a week.

Never keep turtles in an aquarium with fish and snails. The turtles may gobble the others up.

In the wild, turtles hibernate during cold weather. You might release your pet in the early fall so it can bed down as nature intended. Should you decide to keep your shelled friend over the winter, you will notice that it moves slower and eats less.

Feeding. Turtles eat both plants and meat. Land turtles eat mainly plants; water turtles eat mainly meat. Offer land turtles a variety of vegetables and fruits. They need a piece of cuttlebone to gnaw on and a vitamin D supplement twice a week.

Water turtles can swallow only when they are in water. Therefore, place food in their water. Give them earthworms, mealworms, live insects, pieces of raw fish, minced meat, and canned dog food. Because water turtles tend to be messy eaters, remove leftover food to keep your tank clean.

Most turtles eat daily, but some only eat two or three times a week. They usually eat more in summer than in winter.

If a newly captured turtle refuses to eat for more than a week, put it back in the wild where you caught it.

Handling. Because turtles can carry salmonella bacteria (which can cause illness), you must take precautions when handling them. *Always wash your hands after playing with a turtle. Never hold a turtle close to your face* or allow it to breathe in your face. *Don't kiss a turtle.* Stroke it, talk to it, but save your kisses for people.

Never paint your turtle's shell. Paint prevents the shell from growing properly and can seriously damage your pet. If you ever find a turtle with paint on its shell, remove the paint with nail polish remover and cottonballs. *See also:* REPTILES.

W-Y

WILD ANIMALS. Keeping wild animals confined as pets can be dangerous and inhumane. Small mammals, like raccoon, skunks, and opossums, may be cute and gentle when they are youngsters, but when they grow up they become wild and may bite and claw you.

Most baby animals found alone aren't orphans in need of help. Animal parents frequently leave their offspring while they look for food. Unless you are absolutely sure that the parents are dead, leave a young wild animal alone.

Never approach a wild animal that seems friendly. It may act sluggish because it has rabies, a serious disease. If you find an injured animal, call a local wildlife officer, a humane society, or a nature center. Too often animals suffer at the hands of kindhearted people who don't know how to care for them. Also, in may states it is illegal to confine wild animals without a permit.

Because there are people who want exotic pets, like monkeys and cheetahs, animals' mothers are often killed so their babies can be captured. Only about one out of twenty exotic pets live for more than a year in captivity.

Some small wild animals, such as certain insects, reptiles, and amphibians, can make good pets, but the best place to observe wild mammals and birds is where they're happiest—in the wild.

YORKSHIRE TERRIER. Developed in Yorkshire, England, in the mid-nineteenth century, these small spirited dogs have long, silky hair that hangs to the ground. "Yorkies" are loving dogs that easily adapt to city or country living. *See also:* DOGS.

ABOUT THE
AUTHOR

Leda Blumberg lives on a farm near Yorktown Heights, New York, where she trains horses, teaches riding, leads a 4-H group, and cares for her horse, Damascus; her cat, Wanda; and her Irish setter, Ryan. Goats, geese, guinea pigs, and garter snakes have been among her many pets. Leda is a writer, a natural history instructor, and formerly a veterinarian's assistant.